this is how we roll

Team Building Through Conflict Management

WORKPLACE GUIDEBOOK

Nadia Kyba

ISBN: 978-1-9992509-4-2

Printed in Canada

CONTENTS

PART ONE

Conflict: The Way to Success

PART TWO

Moving from Conflict to Cohesion

PART THREE

Your Team's Power Play

PART FOUR

Performing and Beyond

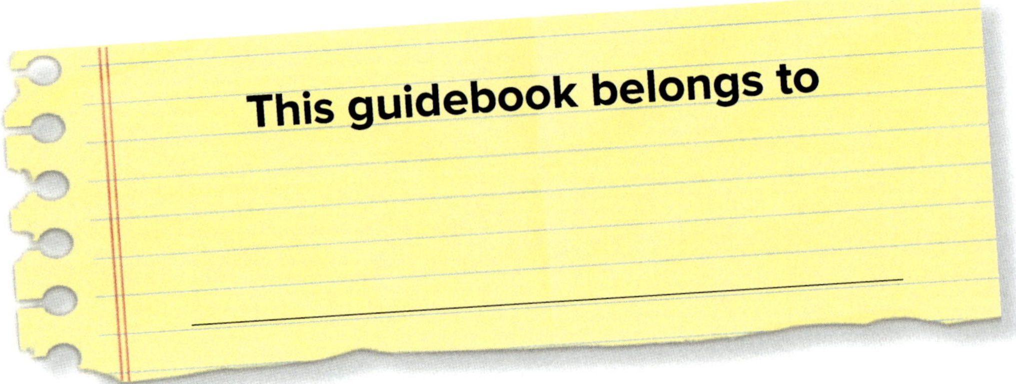

HOW TO USE THIS BOOK

- This is a space designed to be used as a team-building guide, a journal, and a learning tool.
- Write, write, write! Research shows that knowledge is often cemented through writing.
- This book can be used as a team book—a space for your team to record their journey and commitments to one another.
- This book can be used for individual work that can be applied to any life situation.
- Each section ends with an Ah-Ha! page to document insights.

WELCOME!

The goal of this book is to provide you with the knowledge and tools to *anticipate*, *recognize*, *address* and *prevent* conflict. By applying what you learn here and moving from conflict to cohesion, you and your team can grow in ways you've always hoped. Be mindful of your time together doing this work. It is in the small acts and conversations that trust is built. Once you have trust, there are no barriers to what your team can achieve.

I am so excited for you!

Nadia

> "Success is a journey, not a destination. The doing is often more important than the outcome."
>
> —Arthur Ashe*

*Ashe (1943-1993) was an African American professional tennis player, winner of three Grand Slam Titles.

PART ONE

Conflict: The Way to Success

"There is a crack in everything; that's how light gets in."

– Leonard Cohen, Canadian Singer, Songwriter, Poet and Novelist

"I am a woman in process. I'm just trying like everybody else. I try to take every conflict, every experience, and learn from it. Life is never dull."

– Oprah Winfrey, American Media Executive, Producer, Philanthropist

Group Guidelines: How Do We Agree to Be Together?

Teams are made up of members who may have different ideas of what is and isn't acceptable conduct. This can lead to negative behaviors, such as members being late for work, gossiping, or texting during meetings—and will ultimately result in frustration on the part of other team members and leaders. Guidelines establish a baseline for behavior and set group norms. They provide an agreement to refer to if they're not being followed in the future. They should be developed by the group that is agreeing to them—not created as a solo exercise by a team member, leader or board executive. You need your team's buy-in for this to work.

It's a good idea to set up specific guidelines anytime you are working together with a group. Guidelines allow for predictability in these environments and create trust.

TIP: When creating guidelines with your team, try to avoid vague principles such as "Be respectful." These types of phrases mean something different to everyone. Each guideline should be clear and simple. If someone suggests something vague, like "Be respectful," you can say, "Can you tell me what that looks like?" They might answer, "Don't roll your eyes," "Listen before responding," or "Don't interrupt." These clarified meanings will help you and the rest of the team understand what "respect" means to the person suggesting it. The guidelines must also be specific in order for people to know exactly what to do (or not do) to follow them.

This is some of the most important work you'll do as a team. Here are some examples of meeting guidelines I use and have seen used successfully:

1. **Confidentiality** – What is said in the room stays in the room unless everyone agrees to share the information outside the group.

2. **Listen to understand** – When we do this, we are able to hear what our teammates are saying rather than focusing on our own response.

3. **Focus on the future** – An easy rule to apply: Discuss the past *only* if it is to make a plan for the future. This helps avoid prolonged conversations that can sidetrack your group. By focusing on the future, you will ensure your group moves forward.

4. **One person speaks at a time** – Allowing one person at a time to have the floor creates respect within the group and allows for more effective communication.

5. **No blaming or shaming** – Blame tells someone they've done something wrong. Shame exposes them. Both inhibit trust and openness.

6. **Give feedback, not criticism** – Feedback uses strength-based language describing first what is working followed by what isn't. Avoid using the word "but" between the two descriptions, as it tends to negate the first statement.

7. **Take a break if you need one** – Breaks are a powerful tool to use when emotions are running high.

8. **Phones away, in bags or with facilitator** – Phone use during meetings is distracting for everyone.

9. **Allow the facilitator to manage the meeting** (e.g., call breaks if necessary, move people along if going off topic or taking too long)

OUR GROUP GUIDELINES

1.

2.

3.

4.

5.

6.

7.

8.

9.

10

11.

12.

Ask yourself: "What do I need in order to be safe, stay open, be curious and be willing to express new ideas and try new things?"

"Does it pay to listen? Always."

– Arlene Dickinson, Canadian Entrepreneur and Television Personality

Disagreement or Conflict?

Teams who are able to identify conflict early on are better able to manage it prior to escalation. As you prepare to manage conflict effectively, you will learn to recognize the signs of conflict brewing and differentiate between a simple disagreement and deeper conflict.

A disagreement is a minor contrast in opinions. Conflict, on the other hand, is a disagreement with emotions attached. Once a disagreement has become a conflict, it takes active work to resolve.

CONFLICT IS NOT ONLY INEVITABLE; IT'S NECESSARY

Conflict is normal, positive and beneficial for teams. It does not matter how skilled or how friendly the people on your team are, or how long your team has been together; conflict will come up. This predictability is a great thing! Why? Because when you can predict something, you can prevent it or, at the very least, prepare yourself to weather it successfully.

Conflict on a team is like an earthquake: No one wants to think about it, but we all know it is inevitable. So, we buy earthquake kits. We seismically upgrade bridges and schools. Because of this, we poise ourselves for success in the face of disaster.

Some ways conflict can help your team:

- Builds trust
- Teaches people to collaborate
- Allows for consideration of new ideas
- Creates new ways of doing things
- Introduces an issue from a different perspective

NOTES

EXERCISE

Name some of the disagreements you have been involved with that could have escalated to conflict.

In the past, have you been on a team that was able to effectively manage conflict when it came up? How did the team do this?

How about a team that didn't? What happened? What could have been different?

What are some of the ways conflict can benefit your team?

Conflict is neither good nor bad. It is what you do with it that can either benefit your team or not.

"In the midst of chaos, there is also opportunity."

– Sun Tzu, Chinese General, Military Strategist and Writer

Understanding Perception: The Circle of Inference

As humans, we don't have the power to read minds, yet every day we are faced with the task of trying to understand what others are thinking. We do this so we can determine our own actions. When we misinterpret another's motivations based on our own perception of the facts, it can lead to conflict. In simple terms, we jump to conclusions. Human nature leads us to do this hundreds of times a day. This chapter explores why we jump to conclusions and how we can avoid doing so.

THE CIRCLE OF INFERENCE

The Circle of Inference[5] helps us understand the assumptions and decision-making that guide our daily lives. Slowing down our decision-making process by applying this tool can help us make great choices, manage conflict and build relationships.

Facts

A fact is not something that's open to interpretation. It is pure data. It can be observed by anyone.

Selected and Interpreted Facts

Selected facts are the facts we pull (notice or think are important) based on our past experiences, culture, upbringing, state of mind, level of distraction, preferences and tendencies.

Assumptions

Assumptions are what we believe to be true, but are not based on fact. Assumptions are made using the selected facts we take from a situation. They are often made in a split second and occur hundreds of times in a day. They inform our decisions—we analyze information and draw conclusions about reality based on them.

Beliefs

Beliefs are formed once an assumption is made. You can't have a belief without an assumption. A belief is also the foundation for decision-making. Once you arrive at a belief—again, all of this happens in seconds—you move forward with a decision and take an action.

Actions

An action naturally flows out of a decision. We make decisions based on our beliefs.

HOW TO WORK THROUGH THE CIRCLE

Step 1: Start at the top of the circle with the facts.

Ask yourself: *What do I know*? Make a list of every single fact you know—even things that seem insignificant.

Step 2: Review your selected facts.

By virtue of you personally selecting the information you did when you made note of the facts, the information is a list of *selected facts*. Now you need to see if there are any other facts—missed considerations—you may have omitted. As with Step 1, for each selected fact, ask yourself, *How do I know this*? *Are these selected facts based on a core value that I have*? *If so, what is that value, and how does it impact my choice in fact selection*? Go back and look at the facts and look for facts you may have missed. Take note of them.

Step 3: Review the situation for assumptions.

Remember that an assumption is a piece of information that has not been proven to be true or based on facts. List your assumptions. Identify which assumptions are safe assumptions—assumptions for which you have supporting facts.

Step 4: Identify your beliefs.

Ask yourself these questions: *What are my personal beliefs going into this situation*? *What beliefs have I formed based on the facts, the selected facts and the assumptions I have made*? *What do I believe to be true, that might not be*? *What conclusions have I drawn as a result*? *How might my personal values be impacting my conclusions*?

Step 5. Decide on an action and confirm that decision.

Once you have gone through your analysis, make a decision based on what you know are **facts** and **safe assumptions**. Test your decision by checking out viable alternatives. *How would different assumptions create different actions*? *What happens when I try to consider alternate possibilities in my interpretations of the facts*?

EXERCISE

This exercise can be done individually or as a team.

1. Think of a present issue among the team that you'd like to resolve.

Issue ____

2. Go through the Circle of Inference to separate facts from assumptions so the issue can be properly resolved.

Fact ____

Fact ____

Fact ____

Fact ____

Fact ____

Assumption ____

Assumption ____

Assumption____

Assumption ____

Assumption____

3. Now put yourself in the other person's shoes and go through the same process.

Fact____

Fact ____

Fact ____

Fact ____

Fact ____

Assumption ____

Assumption ____

Assumption ____

Assumption ____

Assumption ____

4. What new insights are you seeing about your/your team's decision-making process?

5. How is your team better informed now to take action in this situation?

6. What action(s) will you take next?

Life moves fast, and you often need to make decisions just as quickly, relying on assumptions to do so. Yet as you have now seen, this can be a direct path to conflict if you're not careful. Being aware of this process and using it consistently will allow you to challenge assumptions with your teammates to develop greater understanding and avoid misperceptions.

"Peace is not the absence of conflict but the ability to cope with it."

– Mahatma Gandhi, Social Activist and Political Ethicist

Catching Conflict Early: It's All in the Mush

THE RED FLAGS: HOW DOES CONFLICT START?

Verbal and Non-Verbal Communication

Verbal communication includes words that are spoken, as well as written words—including emails, texts and written letters. Non-verbal communication is any communication that does not involve words. There's a significant body of research about the impact and importance of non-verbal communication. It's been found, through the findings of two studies combined, that 55 percent of communication is body language, 38 percent is tone of voice, and only 7 percent is the actual words spoken.[6] Eye rolling, tone of voice and posture are all non-verbal communicators that can indicate conflict.

Face-to-face verbal communication is not generally problematic, as we can see non-verbal cues and consider them, which helps with avoiding or working through disagreement. Phone communication is also verbal, and, although not as effective as talking face-to-face, we can still hear tone and engage in back-and-forth dialogue. For teams trying to resolve conflict, it is written verbal communication that has been the most devastating.

IT'S ALL IN THE MUSH: HOW CONFLICT ESCALATES

Interpersonal mush is an interaction between two or more people based on stories they have made up about each other but haven't checked out. When these dynamics are present, as time passes, it becomes more and more difficult to determine what is true and what stories have been used to fill in gaps in understanding.

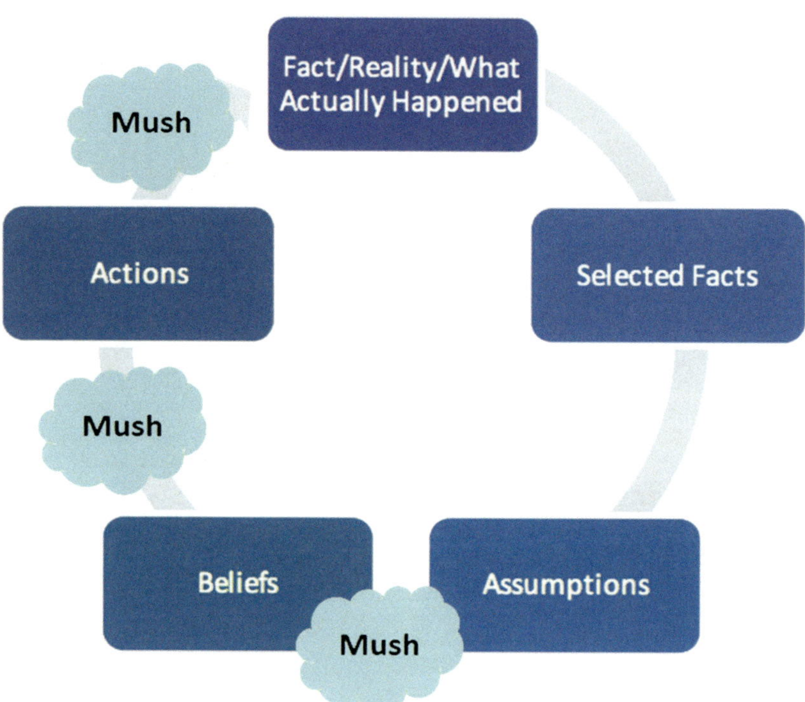

TIP: Practice Your Detective Skills! Non-verbal communication will offer you clues as to possible discord on your team. Watch for when people on your team are caught up in that darned mush, creating stories based on selected facts and assumptions, sharing them (gossip), and applying them to new situations. If you see it, jump on the circle, go back to the FACTS and ask those great clarifying questions. Before you know it, you will be converting conflict to cohesion on your team.

MY PART 1 *ah ha* MOMENTS

PART TWO

Moving from Conflict to Cohesion

"In the middle of difficulty lies opportunity."

– Albert Einstein, Theoretical Physicist

"Sometimes the hardest thing to do is just stay human."

– Michael Franti, American Rapper, Musician, Poet, Activist, Documentarian and Singer-songwriter

Conflict Styles

Each person on your team has a different personality. They also have unique life experiences that shape their style for both displaying and dealing with conflict. No two people on your team will use the exact same conflict style in every circumstance. Consideration of your team members' conflict styles helps you to anticipate how an individual will react in a certain situation. Failure to do this causes ongoing friction and lower levels of success.

Here is a brief list of behaviors you might see for each conflict style, adapted from Kraybill's Conflict Style Inventory.[7]

Avoiding

Avoiders pretend conflict never happened or does not exist. People who use this style are generally uncomfortable with any conflict at all. Behaviors that might indicate this style:

- Not returning challenging emails or phone calls
- Not making eye contact during times of conflict
- Avoiding social events because they are worried about confrontation

Giving in

People who approach conflict this way accommodate or acquiesce to the other person by accepting their point of view, even if it is different from their own. These people are generally viewed as agreeable. It can, however, be difficult to trust them because they do not express their own desires and beliefs. Behaviors that might indicate this style:

- Volunteering for jobs no one else wants to do
- Giving in on a smaller issue in an attempt to resolve a larger conflict
- Putting the concerns of others before their own

Standing your ground

Sometimes this style is necessary. Police officers or doctors need to be able to stand their ground when dealing with conflict. Used at the wrong time, however, this style can escalate conflict. Behaviors of this style include:

- Persuasiveness
- Insistence
- Attacking/being aggressive
- Making demands and controlling situations
- Citing policy or saying, "This is the way we've always done it," as rationale for decisions

Compromising

This style is a step toward converting conflict—people are able to focus on the bigger points and let the smaller points go. The downside is that the parties involved often feel like nobody wins. Behaviors look like:

- Taking turns
- Meeting halfway
- Partially pleasing everyone

Collaborating

Collaborating involves listening to all sides and discussing common interests. This requires thinking creatively to resolve a problem without giving in or compromising. Collaboration values protection of the relationship as a key objective in resolving the conflict. Behaviors look like:

- Having face-to-face conversations
- Moving from positions to interests
- Considering creative ideas
- Thinking outside of the box or policy
- Finding a solution that meets the interests/needs of everyone involved

NOTES

EXERCISE

Team member conflict styles:

Name ______________________________ Conflict Style ___________________________

Name ______________________________ Conflict Style ___________________________

Name ______________________________ Conflict Style ___________________________

Name ______________________________ Conflict Style ___________________________

Name ______________________________ Conflict Style ___________________________

Name ______________________________ Conflict Style ___________________________

Name ______________________________ Conflict Style ___________________________

Name ______________________________ Conflict Style ___________________________

Name ______________________________ Conflict Style ___________________________

Name ______________________________ Conflict Style ___________________________

Name ______________________________ Conflict Style ___________________________

Name ______________________________ Conflict Style ___________________________

Name ______________________________ Conflict Style ___________________________

Name ______________________________ Conflict Style ___________________________

Name ______________________________ Conflict Style ___________________________

Name ______________________________ Conflict Style ___________________________

Name ______________________________ Conflict Style ___________________________

Name ______________________________ Conflict Style ___________________________

What is your predominant conflict style (avoiding, giving in, standing your ground, compromising, or collaborating)?

My predominant conflict style:

Consider the contexts in which you use different conflict styles:

At work:

With your children:

With your partner:

With your close friends:

On your team:

With a person in a position of authority:

How can you begin to apply a collaborative style in each of these contexts?

At work:

With your children:

With your partner:

With your close friends:

On your team:

With a person in a position of authority:

Understanding the conflict styles of your team members is a key component for being able to identify conflict early. It is crucial for leadership to understand the styles of every team member so when issues come up, they are able to spot the dynamics happening right away and support each member as needed.

"Out beyond ideas of wrongdoing and rightdoing there is a field. I'll meet you there."

– Rumi, 13th-century Persian Poet

Positions and Interests: How to Create an All-win

Many of us spend a good portion of our waking hours at work. As such, we invest a lot of emotional energy there. It is not surprising, then, that when conflict comes up, we can be reactive rather than prudent. Conflict happens *between* people—not in isolation. This means it cannot be solved in isolation either. As uncomfortable as it may be sometimes, when a conflict arises, a neutrally facilitated conversation may need to happen among everyone involved. Managing conflict on your team doesn't have to be a win-lose proposition. The key to a win-win outcome is understanding the positions and the interests of each person involved.

Positions are perceived fixed solutions to a problem. A position is typically a stance taken by the party who raises the conflict or takes issue with something.

Interests are what is important to each person involved in the conflict. Positions are based on interests. Interests show us the deeper reasons for the conflict, as well as why those issues are important to them.

THE FIVE STEPS TO CONFLICT RESOLUTION

1. Frame the issue

Name the problem using neutral language. Let's take a look at the examples below:

- Use the words "transparency around decision-making" rather than "biased decisions" or "favoritism."
- Use "tone of voice" rather than "they are always angry."

2. Identify positions

These may be demands, threats, or terms and conditions. For example:

- "If this doesn't happen, I will . . ."
- "I won't be on the committee if ____ is on it."

3. Explore interests

Our interests are what we really want. They are the reason our position is important to us. They are our hopes, feelings, concerns, needs and aspirations.

4. List common interests

Which interests are important to both parties? This is the golden ticket in finding common ground to move forward.

5. Explore options and develop a plan

What options are there that will serve the interests of all parties? How can those options be actioned? Who needs to do what to make change happen?

TIP: As with most conflict, an iceberg is not as simple as it seems. There's a lot going on beneath the surface. By focusing on the problem at the surface level, we ignore what really matters to people.

EXERCISE

Numbers 1 and 2 can be done individually or as a team.

1. Identify an outstanding conflict on your team:

2. To address this issue, run through the Five Steps to Conflict Resolution.

Step 1 - Frame the issue:

Step 2 - Identify the positions of each person involved in the conflict:

Step 3 - Explore interests of yourself and your teammates:

Step 4 - List common interests:

Step 5 - Explore options and develop a plan:

Options:

Plan:

You may also choose to write your answers into a chart. If you are doing this exercise with your team, I'd recommend recreating this chart on large paper in your meetings.

Positions	Interests	Options	Plan

The benefit to getting clear on what positions and interests are at play in any conflict is that once you know the interests of everyone involved, you can speak the language of each person by addressing what is most important to them. This makes it easier to build trust and strengthen bonds, and to find common ground and resolution.

"Do one thing a day that scares you."

– Eleanor Roosevelt, American Political Figure, Diplomat and Activist

Communication for Success

In conflict, face-to-face communication can be scary but is crucial. These conversations can be hard without the proper strategies in mind to minimize damage. In this chapter, we will walk through some helpful tools, as well as scripts and prompts to maximize communication success.

SIX ESSENTIAL QUESTIONS BEFORE YOU EMAIL (OR TEXT, OR DM, OR TWEET)

Sending an email provides a shield that protects us when we are feeling vulnerable and emotional about an issue and potential responses. But does it solve anything? Almost never. Many years of experience in conflict management has proven that sending emails is quite possibly the *number one factor in the escalation and prolonging of a conflict or dispute*. Before you email (or text, DM, or tweet) ask yourself:

1. Is it important?
2. Do you need to apologize?
3. Have you waited too long to respond?
4. Do you anticipate questions?
5. Is it complicated?
6. Is it personal?

If you answered yes to any of the questions above, you should consider face-to-face communication.

TRICKY CONVERSATION STARTER SCRIPT

The following script, modeled after Rosenberg's nonviolent communication process, takes you through five steps to poise your conversation for success while creating a dialogue that is free of blame or shame.[8]

1. **Acknowledge**. Thank the other person for being willing to talk.
2. **Observation**. "I heard..." "I saw..." Describe the problem starting with "I."
3. **Feeling**. "I feel..." Describe how the problem is making you feel.
4. **Need**. Explain what you need in order to feel better about the problem.
5. **Request**. "Would you be willing to...?" Suggest a solution that would benefit both of you.

Pay particular attention to the second point—FEELING. In this point you need to really stop and think about how the behavior that you describe in Point 1 made you feel. It can be disappointed, sad, hurt, left out. Saying, "I feel that when you ____, it is not fair" is not describing what you're feeling. Most people get tripped up on this point, but it is crucial to the whole conversation.

DURING THE CONVERSATION

- Be descriptive
- Clarify and ask questions
- Show empathy
- Avoid shame and blame

TIP: Bring a piece of paper with some examples of great open-ended questions (questions that can't be answered with yes or no) to have at your fingertips during the conversation. Here are some examples:
"Help me to understand" or *"What does that look like?"*
"What's on your mind?"
"What am I missing?" or "Tell me more."

EXERCISE

Your turn. Prepare for a tricky conversation you need to have.

Why is this conversation important to me?

Why might this conversation be important to the other person?

What are the key issues? Have I framed them in a neutral way?

What is my position?

What is the position of the other person?

What are my interests?

What might their interests be?

What assumptions am I making (Circle of Inference—check the facts)?

What are some possible negatives coming out of the conversation?

How can I set the stage for success? Where will we meet?

How will I invite the other person to the conversation? Email, face to face, text or phone?

Fill in the below five statements for your conversation starter script:

Acknowledge:

Observation:

Feeling:

Need:

Request:

MY PART 2 *ah ha* MOMENTS

PART THREE

Your Team's Power Play

"There is no limit to what we can accomplish."

– Michelle Obama, American Lawyer, University Administrator, Writer and Former First Lady of the United States

"Chemistry kind of builds all season. It's not like we say, 'OK, it's game one, and now we've got our chemistry.' I think it shifts and moves all season long."

– Nick Nurse, Head Coach, Toronto Raptors Basketball

The Stages of Team Development

Although most would say they dislike conflict and try to avoid it, conflict is inevitable in any team. An amazing byproduct of conflict resolution is that as a team moves through conflict and resolves issues together, they become better together. They produce better results and experience greater success. The best way for this to happen is to anticipate conflict and prepare for it as you would with any storm.

THE FOUR STAGES OF GROUP DEVELOPMENT

One way to anticipate conflict is to track your team through the four stages of group development: forming, storming, norming and performing.[9] Each stage is inevitable and necessary for team growth on the way to optimal performance. It is crucial for teams poised for success to understand where they are, where they want to go and how they are going to manage roadblocks that will come up at each stage.

Forming

This is the first stage of team formation where people come together to work toward a common goal or task. Although every team or group is made up of leaders and members with unique personalities and conflict styles that have been shaped by their life experiences, it is the common goal that makes a team, a team. During this stage, you will see politeness and no risk-taking.

Storming

The storming phase begins after the team has been together for a while—anywhere from 4–8 weeks—and has been through some high-pressure situations, such as tight deadlines or budget cuts. During this phase, personality differences start to bump up against each other and relationships become strained. Already-established cliques become further entrenched. Some team members start to question authority. If there is a lack of alignment on team goals and processes, unmanaged conflict starts to show up.

Norming

Teams that accept and anticipate conflict are able to move to the norming stage. This is when conversations start to happen and trust is slowly built. Issues are named and discussed. Transparency with decision-making starts to happen between leadership and team members. Team members align on the team goal, which becomes the primary focus. Cliques are broken down in order to work together. Different personality styles are acknowledged and accepted.

This stage can be prolonged because as new situations arise, the team can revert back to storming and old habits as they navigate their way.

Performing

In this stage, conflict is no longer feared or avoided. There is general understanding that things may get hairy or unpleasant, but the team is aligned on their mission. The team goals come before anything else, including individual egos (the need to be right) or the general adversity that inevitably arises. New team members are able to come and go smoothly. Although the new team will again move through the four stages, the movement is more fluid because of the culture that has been built. There is a driving confidence that the team will stay intact.

Anticipation is everything. Every member of your team, and those involved with the team, can be better equipped for success if they go in with their eyes wide open. Keep the channel of communication open and, as a group, identify your current stage. As you move through these stages, be sure to stop and celebrate—because once you expand beyond a stage, you are one step closer to performing.

WHERE IS YOUR TEAM?

Moving between each of the four categories, answer the following questions:

STAGE	1. How will we know we are here? (What behaviors will we see?)	2. How can we move on to the next stage?
FORMING		
STORMING		
NORMING		
PERFORMING		

Discuss answers with your team.

"Lead from the back and let others believe they are in front."
– Nelson Mandela, South African Anti-apartheid Revolutionary, Political Leader and Philanthropist

PEER LEADERSHIP: Cultivating Leaders to Mitigate Conflict

Peer leaders can be counted on to bring individuals together to reinforce the strength of a team. They are also often the ones to support teammates in addressing conflict when it comes up. They engage with each member of the team. They recognize the importance of building strong relationships. Once there is a foundation for deeper connection, teams are able to collaborate to work toward common goals.

HOW CAN WE AS A TEAM CULTIVATE PEER LEADERS?

1. Establish mentorship opportunities.

Setting up mentorship relationships on your team can give your team members a chance to lead by example. Mentors pass their knowledge on to the next group coming up behind them.

2. Give them a job.

It can be any job. Sharing the responsibility of running your team gives its members insight into the moving parts. Give each member responsibilities to enable confidence building.

3. Help them lead by example.

Leaders should be the hardest workers out there. They set the tone for the team's work ethic. Have your leaders facilitate meetings, lead lunch & learns and represent the team at workshops or conferences.

4. Set up empowerment circles.

Effective leaders leverage diversity on their team by empowering members to express and embrace their own unique strengths. You can encourage your teammates to do this. One way is to rotate team members in leading empowerment circles each week at team meetings. In the circle, have each team member share with the group what they think they did well that week. Explain that the answers should be strength based, meaning they should focus on something positive they did, not something they didn't do. This activity only takes about 10 minutes, and the benefits will amaze you.

5. Walk the talk.

Don't expect peers to respect leaders who don't model best practices themselves. Leaders communicate effectively and are transparent. They don't gossip but offer feedback. For example, if you want your team to deal with conflict face to face, don't send texts and emails yourself. If you model solid leadership skills at all times, your team leaders will follow suit and new leaders will emerge.

6. Teach empathy.

Empathy drives connection and is the foundation to building strong teams with strong leadership. Empathy is understanding another's emotion. The key to empathy is being able to listen without passing judgment, giving advice or pointing out the bright side. Just listen.

7. Train team members to lead conflict resolution meetings.

Once you have an individual or two you think are ready for this level of leadership, walk them through what it would look like to lead meetings and conversations for conflict resolution. Teach them the Circle of Inference and the Five Steps to Conflict Resolution. You'll be surprised how quickly team members will pick this stuff up and settle into using these tools.

EXERCISE

How do you support peer leadership?

1. Who on your team stands out as a leader to you? What job(s) can you give them to develop their leadership skills?

2. What ideas from this chapter will you implement now in order to encourage leadership among all your team members?

3. Transparency with team roles and responsibilities goes a long way in mitigating conflict and creating cohesion. If you haven't started this work yet, make a list of all the roles on your team. For each role, map out the responsibilities associated with it. What specific responsibilities are associated with each leadership role? What is required for people to move into those roles? You can do this work independently or with your team.

Peer leadership is the oil that smooths the interpersonal inner workings of a team.

"Connection is the energy that exists between people when they feel seen, heard, and valued; when they can give and receive without judgment; and when they derive sustenance and strength from the relationship."

– Brené Brown, Research Professor at the University of Houston, Chair at The Graduate College of Social Work

Team Purpose, Goals and Values

For your team to function at its highest potential, every team member must have a clear, shared understanding of why you are together and what is important to each individual member. Once your team's shared purpose, goals and values are identified, they can serve as a compass for every aspect of your time together.

TEAM PURPOSE STATEMENT (MOTTO):

Your team's purpose is its raison d'être—its reason for being. Some teams create a motto as a purpose statement; for example: "When they go low we go high," Michelle Obama campaign; "Impossible is Nothing," Adidas; "North Over Everything," Toronto Raptors. **Write yours below**:

TEAM GOALS:

When a team is aligned on their goals, they are much more likely to reach them. These usually involve performance outcomes, such as what your team is working toward.

1.

2.

3.

VALUES

Our values are linked to our interests. They are what is important to us and what make us tick. They impact our perception of the world.

- Dependability
- Reliability
- Loyalty
- Commitment
- Open-mindedness
- Consistency
- Honesty
- Efficiency
- Innovation
- Humility
- Fairness
- Justice
- Hard work
- Punctuality
- Family
- Creativity
- Good humor
- Collaboration
- Integrity
- Adaptability
- Professionalism
- Service
- Volunteerism
- Growth
- Balance
- Courage
- Reliability
- Transparency
- Relationships
- Compassion
- Adventure
- Motivation
- Positivity
- Optimism
- Passion
- Respect
- Fitness
- Education
- Perseverance
- Trust
- Service
- Environmentalism
- Excellence
- Fun

MY TOP 3 VALUES

1.

2.

3.

MY TEAM'S VALUES

Name ______________________ Values ______________________

Name ______________________ Values ______________________

Name ______________________ Values ______________________

Name ______________________ Values ______________________

Name ______________________ Values ______________________

Name ______________________ Values ______________________

Name ______________________ Values ______________________

Name ______________________ Values ______________________

Name ______________________ Values ______________________

Name ______________________ Values ______________________

Name ______________________ Values ______________________

Name ______________________ Values ______________________

Name ______________________ Values ______________________

Name ______________________ Values ______________________

Name ______________________ Values ______________________

Name ______________________ Values ______________________

Name ______________________ Values ______________________

Name ______________________ Values ______________________

Name ______________________ Values ______________________

Name ______________________ Values ______________________

Name ______________________ Values ______________________

MY TEAM'S COMMON VALUES

Value: ______________________________ x ____

Value: ______________________________ x ____

Value: ______________________________ x ____

Value: ______________________________ x ____

Value: ______________________________ x ____

Value: ______________________________ x ____

Value: ______________________________ x ____

Value: ______________________________ x ____

Value: ______________________________ x ____

Value: ______________________________ x ____

OUR TEAM'S TOP VALUES (CHOOSE 3 TO 5)

Value	Definition

What actions will your team take inside and outside the boardroom to fully embody your team values? How can you start some of these initiatives? Who on your team can take the lead?

For example:

Action: Our team will execute an annual fundraiser for the local food bank.

Lead: Jazmine (Community Outreach Committee chair)

Value: Compassion, volunteerism

Action:	Lead:	Value:
Action:	Lead:	Value:
Action:	Lead:	Value:
Action:	Lead:	Value:
Action:	Lead:	Value:
Action:	Lead:	Value:

TIP: When teams take the time to learn the values of each member, great things happen. Any team is not homogeneous, and that's a good thing. It's our differences that make us stronger. The secret sauce is naming each person's values and respecting differences.

Once your team is able to articulate your shared purpose, goals and values, there will be no stopping you!

NOTES

MY PART 3 *ah ha* MOMENTS

PART FOUR

Performing and Beyond

"I think, team first. It allows me to succeed, and it allows my team to succeed."

– Lebron James, Champion NBA Player and Philanthropist

"The will to win means nothing without the will to prepare."

– Juma Ikangaa, Tanzanian Champion Marathon Runner

Team Planning Meetings: Your Team's Power Play

Team planning meetings provide a structured format to focus on surfacing issues and can be used for whatever challenge your team is facing at any given time. Having the same structure for the meetings every week is important, as it provides consistency to aid in establishing predictability, safety and trust.

Once you have established predictability, you can use the meetings to help with conflict in a variety of ways, such as sharing information, dealing with specific conflicts and checking in with the team. The key is that the meetings don't just occur when problems come up; they are predictable and regular. Then, when challenging conversations are required, there is already a set forum in which to hold them.

A FORUM FOR MITIGATING AND RESOLVING CONFLICT

1. Sharing important, potentially conflictual information
2. Addressing specific concerns that have come up
3. As a regular forum for checking in

DURING THE MEETING

The meetings should be an hour long and, for best results, should happen in a private space. If at all possible, have a neutral facilitator. This could be rotated between team members or someone who has some experience chairing meetings—someone who is universally respected.

TEAM PLANNING MEETING OUTLINE

Here is a sample team meeting timeline.

Introduction of facilitator (if applicable)	3 minutes
Icebreaker	7 minutes
Review of Guidelines	5 minutes (This will need 15 minutes or more during your first meeting[s] when the guidelines are being established. You can adjust the rest of your timeline accordingly.)
What is working well?	10 minutes
What are we worried about?	15 minutes
Options/Ideas	10 minutes
Plan	10 minutes (Choose who will document and send out the plan summary during this time.)

PITFALLS TO AVOID

- Shaming and blaming
- Facilitator bias
- Skipping meetings
- Giving up
- Missing or ignoring conflict
- Trying to fill the gaps in conversation
- Gossip
- "Pre-and-post-meeting" meetings (when select team members meet on their own)

MONTHLY TEAM PLANNING MEETING SCHEDULE

Be sure to start and end the meetings on time. This creates predictability and accountability. If you don't get through your whole agenda, bring forward items to the next meeting.

"Coming together is a beginning, staying together is progress and working together is success."

– Henry Ford, American Industrialist and Founder of Ford Motor Company

Your Team's Blueprint for Success

Now it's time to create your team's blueprint—a transparent, living document of best practices that you will adjust as needed. Your blueprint is essentially a documented set of systems that you and your team will follow. Each of the pieces involves your team considering both individual and collective needs. The very creation and assessment of these systems will build team cohesion and strengthen communication.

OUR TEAM BLUEPRINT

WHO WE ARE

Purpose/Motto:

Shared Goals:

Shared Values:

HOW WE GROW TOGETHER

Leadership Training:

Mentorship Training:

HOW WE ARE TOGETHER

Team Guidelines:

Communication:

NOTES

Your team's blueprint can be referred to when there are questions or concerns about decision-making. It can (and should!) be reviewed at regular intervals through the year to see what worked and what didn't.

Some Final Thoughts . . .

I've painted a broad picture for you of the steps it takes to convert conflict to cohesion and nudge your team to the performing stage. You now know how important communication is and how to be aware of your own assumptions. You know how to identify non-verbal communication clues in detecting conflict and how to recognize when your team is experiencing interpersonal mush. You have a strong foundation in understanding what's going on around you. Being equipped with this knowledge puts you ahead of 99 percent of teams out there.

Bringing this knowledge and awareness to life in regular team planning meetings and powerful face-to-face interactions will catapult your team forward when it comes to turning any conflict into an opportunity for growth. Combining these pathways for communication with a created team purpose/motto, a shared team goal and team values in which everyone is invested, gives you a unique brand that will enable your team to be recognized anywhere.

Above all, don't give up. Now you have the recipe to make history!

I would love to hear from you. Please reach out to share stories of your team. It's your stories that fill my bucket!

Nadia

nadia@nowwhatfacilitation.com

@nowwhatfacilitation

About Nadia Kyba

Nadia Kyba is the author of *This is How We Roll: A Coach's Guide to Transforming Conflict into High Performance* and the *This Is How We Roll Sports Guidebook*. Nadia been working in the field of Alternative Dispute Resolution for over 20 years. Her passion for training and conflict management has led her to design and facilitate workshops for business organizations, sports associations and families to address individual and group conflict. Nadia's tried-and-tested conflict management strategies can be applied to any team or group.

Nadia Kyba is Founder and President of Now What Facilitation.

Is conflict preventing your team from moving forward? If your team is struggling to work effectively together, and you're spending too much time micromanaging disagreement, it might be time for some intervention. A Now What Workshop can equip your team to work better together. Using the principles found in this guidebook, an experienced facilitator will give you a fun and unique experience, making your team stronger and ready for success. For more information, speaking inquiries and bookings, please visit **www.nowwhatfacilitation.com**.

Endnotes

1 Van Edwards, Vanessa. *Captivate: The Science of Succeeding with People*. New York, New York: Portfolio, an imprint of Penguin Random House, 2017.

2 Karcher, Michael. "Cross-Age Peer Mentoring." *Research in Action*, vol. 7. Alexandria, Virginia: MENTOR/National Mentoring Partnership, 2007

3 Rosenberg, Marshall B. *Nonviolent Communication: A Language of Life*. United States of America: PuddleDancer Press, 2015.

4 Cambridge Dictionary. "Blueprint." Accessed June 20, 2019. https://dictionary.cambridge.org/dictionary/english/blueprint.

5 Senge, Peter M. The Fifth Discipline: The Art and Practice of the Learning Organization. United States of America: Doubleday, 2006.

6 Thompson, Jeff . "Is Nonverbal Communication a Numbers Game?" *Psychology Today*, September 30, 2011. https://www.psychologytoday.com/ca/blog/beyond-words/201109/is-nonverbal-communication-numbers-game.

7 Kraybill, Thomas. *Style Matters: The Kraybill Conflict Style Inventory.* Harrisonburg, Virginia: Riverhouse ePress, 2011.

8 Rosenberg, Marshall B. *Nonviolent Communication: A Language of Life*. United States of America: PuddleDancer Press, 2015.

9 Wikipedia. "Tuckman's Stages of Group Development." Last Modified July 1, 2019. https://en.wikipedia.org/wiki/Tuckman%27s_stages_of_group_development.

Made in the USA
Monee, IL
08 June 2020

32138828R00045